W9-BKB-909

A handy little how-to book
to turn your budding chef
loose in the kitchen.

A Country Store In Your Mailbox®

Gooseberry Patch
600 London Road
P.O. Box 190
Delaware, OH 43015

www.gooseberrypatch.com

1•800•854•6673

Copyright 2006, Gooseberry Patch
1-933494-04-2
First Printing, June, 2006

All rights reserved. No part of this book
may be reproduced or utilized in any form
or by any means, electronic or mechanical,
including photocopying and recording,
or by any information storage and
retrieval system, without permission
in writing from the publisher.

Dedication…

A terrifically tasty cookbook
dedicated to kids and
their grown-ups!

A Big Thank You…

Thanks to kids everywhere. You make us
giggle and fill our days with sunshine!

Table of Contents

Breakfast

Anytime Snack

Yummy treats...easy to make, easy to eat!

Dinnertime

Desserts

Just for Fun

A sundae for **breakfast?** You bet!

Breakfast Banana
SPLit

Breakfast

Serves 1.

VROOM
Start to Finish:
15 minutes

Did You know...?

Blueberries were once called *starfruit* because of the small star shape on the top of every berry.

Ingredients

1 banana

1/2 cup your favorite crunchy cereal, divided

 YUM

1/2 cup fruit-flavored yogurt

1/4 cup blueberries or strawberries, sliced

 1/4 cup pineapple chunks, drained

maraschino cherries (optional)

Tool Kit

butter knife ★ cereal bowl ★ spoon
measuring cups

*Remember...it's a good idea to get your tools out and make sure you have all the ingredients **before** starting.*

Peel banana and cut down the middle lengthwise with a butter knife.

Place banana in a cereal bowl or a banana split dish.

Sprinkle half of the cereal over the banana, but save the other half for sprinkling on top.

Spoon yogurt over the banana and cereal.

Add the rest of the cereal and fruit on top. Add cherries, if you like.

Serves 3 to 4.

tic toc

Start to Finish:
30 minutes

Here's A tip...

French toast sticks are yummy dunked in syrup, but try topping 'em with fruit jam, apple butter, whipped cream, cinnamon-sugar or even warm pie filling!

Q: Why is the sun so bright?

A: It always pays attention in class and does its homework!

French Toast Sticks

Ingredients

6 slices of bread

2 eggs

1/2 cup milk

1/4 teaspoon sugar

1/4 teaspoon cinnamon

1 tablespoon oil

Garnishes: maple syrup, powdered sugar or cream cheese

Tool Kit

kitchen scissors ★ whisk ★ mixing bowl
measuring cups & spoons ★ skillet or griddle
potato masher ★ spatula

This recipe uses the stovetop and hot burners, so be sure to ask an adult for help.

Cut each bread slice into 3 or 4 sticks using kitchen scissors.

Beat eggs with a whisk in a mixing bowl and then mix in milk, sugar and cinnamon.

Dunk each bread stick into the mixture one at a time, letting the bread soak up the egg.

Spread oil on a hot griddle or skillet. Add bread sticks and fry over medium heat for 2 to 3 minutes.

Squish with a potato masher gently so each piece is crispy in the center without burning the crust.

Flip with a spatula when crispy on one side; repeat on the other side.

Dip in maple syrup, sprinkle with powdered sugar or spread with cream cheese.

3 French hens

Spoon batter into cookie cutters to make fun pancake shapes! Give it a try using hearts, stars or gingerbread man cutters. Add a clip-on style clothespin to the cutter so it is easy to lift off a hot griddle or skillet.

Little Squirt pancakes

Ingredients

 1 egg  1/2 cup milk

2 tablespoons butter, melted

 1 cup all-purpose flour

2 teaspoons baking powder

 2 tablespoons sugar

1/2 teaspoon salt

non-stick vegetable spray

Tool Kit

mixing bowl ⭑ whisk ⭑ measuring cups & spoons
funnel ⭑ squirt bottles ⭑ skillet or griddle ⭑ spatula

If too much pancake batter gets in the tip of the squirt bottle, just use a toothpick to open it up again.

Whisk
egg, milk and butter together in a mixing bowl.

Combine
flour, baking powder, sugar and salt and pour into the egg mixture. Stir just enough to wet the flour.

Pour
batter into plastic squirt bottles using the funnel if you need to.

Squirt
batter into sprayed skillet or onto griddle over medium heat and draw shapes, letters or even animals.

Cook
on one side until the bubbles stop popping. Flip and continue cooking briefly on the second side until golden.

Breakfast

Makes 4 cups.

Start to Finish:
45 minutes

Did You know...?

You could spoon Sunny Honey Granola into a sports bottle to take along on a field trip or a family hike?

So handy!

A to-go snack that is great
for the game, after school & camp-outs.

Sunny Honey Granola

Ingredients

2 cups rolled oats

1/2 cup slivered almonds

1/2 cup sunflower seeds

1/2 cup coconut   1/2 cup honey

1/2 cup oil   1/4 cup raisins

non-stick vegetable spray

Tool Kit

measuring cups ✴ mixing bowls ✴ spoon
baking sheet

If you open the oven door to take a peek,
close it quickly to keep the oven hot.

Mix oats, almonds, sunflower seeds and coconut in a mixing bowl.

Stir honey and oil together in a separate bowl and then combine with oat mixture.

Spread out on a sprayed baking sheet and bake at 300 degrees for 20 to 30 minutes, or until golden.

Pour into a clean bowl and stir in raisins.

Breakfast

Serves 2 to 4.

tic toc

Start to Finish:
30 minutes

Did You know...?

This recipe originally came from England? It gets its name because the egg looks as if it's

peeking

out of a hole!

No toads here,

just an egg-cellent breakfast recipe!

ToAd in the Hole

Ingredients

 4 slices bread

non-stick vegetable spray

 4 eggs

salt and pepper to taste

Tool Kit

cutting board ⋆ juice glass ⋆ skillet ⋆ spatula

*Keep floors free of slippery spots by having a
damp cloth handy to wipe up spills.*

Spray both sides of bread with non-stick vegetable spray and place on cutting board.

Cut a hole in the middle of each slice of bread using the juice glass and keep the circles you cut out.

Toast bread slices and circles in a skillet over medium heat for 2 minutes on each side.

Crack an egg into the hole of each bread slice and cook another 2 to 3 minutes, or until eggs are set. Use a spatula to flip and cook second side one to 2 minutes. Sprinkle with salt and pepper, if you like.

Place completed toads-in-the-hole on serving plates and top each with a bread circle so it looks like your "toad" is peeking out!

Breakfast

Makes one dozen.

Start to Finish: 30 minutes

Jam Surprise Muffins

Ingredients

2 cups all-purpose flour (not those!)

 3 tablespoons sugar

1 tablespoon baking powder

 1/2 teaspoon salt

3/4 cup butter, softened

1 egg 1 cup milk

non-stick vegetable spray

 1/2 cup your favorite jam

Not just for breakfast...make 'em mini using a mini muffin tin. A sweet pop-in-your-mouth anytime snack!

Tool Kit

measuring cups & spoons ★ mixing bowls
fork ★ whisk ★ spoon ★ muffin tin
paper liners (optional)

16

Hot muffin tins can ruin a countertop. Be sure to set them on a wire cooling rack or potholder to cool.

Combine flour, sugar, baking powder, and salt in a mixing bowl.

Blend in butter using a fork until mixture is crumbly. Form a well in the center.

Whisk together the egg and milk and then pour into the well in the dry ingredients.

Stir just until ingredients are moistened, about 25 strokes. Batter will be lumpy.

Fill sprayed and floured muffin cups or paper liners about 1/3 full.

Spoon one tablespoon jam on top of batter and cover with enough batter to fill muffin cups 2/3 full.

Bake at 425 degrees for 20 to 25 minutes.

Deliciously Dippable Fondue

Here's A tip...

Fondue is a super sleepover treat...ask friends to bring along their favorite dippers like marshmallows, pretzel rods, strawberries and bananas to share.

Ingredients

1 cup chocolate chips

4 tablespoons milk

 pineapple, pear and apple slices

brownie and angel food cake cubes

marshmallows

pretzel sticks for skewers

Tool Kit

microwave-safe bowl ★ measuring cups & spoons
paring knife ★ wooden spoon

When you're ready to remove hot bowls from the microwave, always use a thick, dry potholder.

Combine
chocolate chips and milk in a microwave-safe bowl.

Cook
in microwave for one minute on high. Stir, then microwave for another 30 seconds.

Skewer
fruit, cake or marshmallows on the pretzel sticks and serve.

Lick all the fondue-palooza

Anytime Snack

Serves 4 to 6.

Start to Finish:
15 minutes

Turn a pizza bagel into a monster for Halloween. Green olive slices become eyes and a banana pepper ring makes an eerie open mouth...add a black olive wedge for the nose!

Bagel Pizzas

Ingredients

4 sliced bagels

8 tablespoons pizza or spaghetti sauce

1/2 cup shredded mozzarella cheese

 your favorite pizza toppings

1 teaspoon Italian seasoning (optional)

Tool Kit

measuring cups & spoons ★ baking sheet ★ spoon

Ask for help with the oven and keep an eye on these little pizzas...the broiler cooks much faster than the oven!

Place each bagel half on a baking sheet.

Spread one tablespoon of sauce on each bagel half.

Sprinkle cheese evenly on top of the sauce.

Add your favorite toppings and Italian seasoning, if you like.

Broil bagels for 5 to 7 minutes, or until cheese is melted and golden.

Anytime Snack

Serves 4 to 6.

Start to Finish:
30 minutes

Just for fun,
serve this up in a
fruit bowl. Slice
an orange in half
and scoop out
the fruit with a
spoon. Fill the
hollowed-out
orange with fruit
dip and tuck in a
paper umbrella!

Knock, Knock. Who's there?
Dewey. Dewey, who?
Dewey have to wait long to eat?

Tropical Whip
fruit dip!

Ingredients

1 cup cream cheese, softened

1 cup pineapple yogurt

1 cup whipped topping

1/4 cup coconut

1/4 cup chopped pecans

Fruit, pretzels or cookies for dipping

Tool Kit

measuring cups ★ mixing bowl
electric mixer ★ wooden spoon

22

Add a few drops of food coloring to
the whipped topping for a splash of color!

Beat cream cheese with an electric mixer on low until fluffy.

Add yogurt a little at a time, blending with mixer on low.

Fold in whipped topping, coconut and pecans and stir well.

Chill at least 15 minutes before serving.

Serves 4.

Start to Finish:
45 minutes

Q: What did the snake say when he was offered a piece of cheese for dinner?

A: Thank you, I'll just have a slither.

Fiesta Nachos!

Ingredients

1/2 pound ground beef

1 teaspoon chili powder

1 teaspoon cumin

1/2 cup onion, chopped

10-oz. bag tortilla chips

2 cups shredded Cheddar cheese

1/2 cup tomato, chopped

1/4 cup black olives, chopped

Garnishes: salsa, sour cream and guacamole

Here's a tip...

Tortilla chips can be found in fun colors. Mix up a bowl of yellow and orange ones for Halloween. How about combining red and blue for the 4th of July?

Tool Kit

measuring cups & spoons ⋆ paring knife ⋆ skillet
wooden spoon ⋆ colander ⋆ 2-quart casserole dish

Before using a knife to chop the onion, it's always a good idea to have an adult close by to help out or answer questions.

Crumble ground beef in a skillet. Add seasonings and chopped onion and stir well.

Cook beef and onion over medium heat until no pink remains and onions are soft. Drain using a colander.

Layer tortilla chips, seasoned beef and cheese in an ungreased casserole dish. Add tomato and olives. Repeat until all ingredients are used.

Bake at 375 degrees for 10 to 20 minutes, or until cheese is melted. Serve warm with salsa, sour cream and guacamole.

What dog will laugh at any joke?

A chi·ha·ha!

tee hee

Anytime Snack

Serves 2 to 4.

Start to Finish:
30 minutes

Here's a tip...

On family game night, serve bread sticks crossed like a *tic-tac-toe* game!

Pepperoni Pizza
Bread sticks

Ingredients

10-oz. tube refrigerated garlic bread sticks

1 cup pizza sauce, divided

4-oz. pkg. pepperoni slices

3/4 cup shredded mozzarella cheese

non-stick vegetable spray

Tool Kit
measuring cups ★ baking sheet ★ spoon

A sheet of wax paper is a good cover-up for microwave-safe containers so food doesn't spatter as it cooks.

Place bread sticks in single layer on a lightly sprayed baking sheet.

Spread about a spoonful of sauce on each bread stick.

Top each with 4 to 5 slices pepperoni and sprinkle with mozzarella cheese.

Bake at 375 degrees for 8 to 10 minutes, or until bread sticks are golden.

Heat remaining pizza sauce in the microwave until warm. Serve with bread sticks for dipping.

pup · a · roni

Baked French Fries

Anytime Snack

Serves 2 to 4.

tic toc

Start to Finish:
1 hour

Did You Know...?

It's tater time...potatoes used to be grown for only their decorative flowers...people thought the potato itself was poisonous. Today, they're the world's most popular veggie!

Ingredients

3 potatoes

1 tablespoon oil

salt to taste

non-stick
vegetable spray

Tool Kit

vegetable brush ★ paring knife ★ mixing bowl
measuring spoons ★ baking sheet ★ spatula

When opening the oven to turn the fries,
always wear an oven mitt.

Scrub potatoes using a vegetable brush.

Cut potatoes into 1/2-inch thick sticks by first slicing potatoes and then stacking the slices, about 3 at a time, to cut into sticks.

Toss potato sticks with oil and salt in a mixing bowl until evenly coated.

Place on a sprayed baking sheet in a single layer.

Bake at 475 degrees for 15 minutes.

Flip fries with spatula carefully. Continue to bake about 25 minutes, or until golden and crispy.

Sprinkle with additional salt to taste and serve.

celebrity
spuds!

Anytime Snack

Makes one dozen.

Start to Finish: 45 minutes

Have some fun! Before baking, it's so easy to twist pretzel dough into your initials, a heart or X's and O's

Twist and shout!

Sweet Pretzel Twists

Ingredients

11-oz. tube refrigerated bread sticks

 2 tablespoons butter, melted

1-1/2 tablespoons sugar

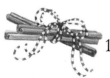 1/2 tablespoon cinnamon

Tool Kit

measuring spoons ★ ruler ★ baking sheet
basting brush

Before beginning any recipe, wash your hands in lots of warm, soapy water, then dry well.

Separate bread sticks and roll each one into an 18-inch rope.

Shape each rope into a circle, overlapping ends by 4 inches

Twist ends together and fold over to form a pretzel shape.

Place pretzels in a single layer on an ungreased baking sheet.

Brush each with butter and then sprinkle with sugar and cinnamon.

Bake at 350 degrees for 15 to 18 minutes.

Anytime Snack

Serves 2 to 4.

tic toc

Start to Finish:
30 minutes

MakeA master-piece!

Make your roll-up unique! Everyone can add their favorite fillings... ham & pineapple, taco meat & salsa, corned beef & Swiss cheese or pepperoni & mushrooms.

Ham & Cheese

roLL-UPS

Ingredients

3 to 4 slices of ham from the deli

4 refrigerated crescent rolls

3 to 4 teaspoons mustard

 1/4 cup shredded Cheddar cheese

Tool Kit

measuring cups & spoons ⋆ kitchen scissors
baking sheet

An apron is a terrific way to keep spills and stains off clothes.

Cut ham into small pieces using kitchen scissors.

Unroll crescent rolls on an ungreased baking sheet.

Pull apart the dough triangles on the dotted lines.

Spoon a little mustard onto each triangle.

Sprinkle each roll with one tablespoon cheese and one tablespoon ham.

Roll triangles up, starting from the long side.

Bake at 350 degrees for 11 to 13 minutes or until rolls are golden.

Q: What do you call cheese that isn't yours?

A: Not 'cho cheese.

CHEESE

Dinnertime

Serves 2 to 4.

tic toc

Start to Finish:
45 minutes

Here's A tip...

Try 'em for breakfast! Scrambled eggs, grated cheese, sausage or bacon make these *quesadillas* worth getting out of bed for.

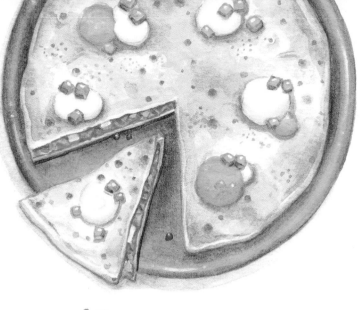

Easy Cheesy Quesadillas

Ingredients

1 cup cooked chicken, shredded

 2 tablespoons onion, chopped

1/4 cup diced green chiles

 1/4 cup salsa or taco sauce

4 flour tortillas

1 cup shredded Monterey Jack cheese

Additional salsa, sour cream and guacamole (optional)

Tool Kit

measuring cups & spoons ★ skillet ★ paring knife
wooden spoon ★ baking sheet

34

Spoons that are made of metal can get hot quickly when stirring food on the stove. It's best to use wooden or plastic spoons.

Combine chicken, onion, chiles and salsa in a deep skillet.

Heat chicken mixture over medium heat for 5 minutes, or until onions are soft. Stir mixture occasionally.

Place 2 tortillas side-by-side on an ungreased baking sheet.

Spoon half the chicken mixture onto each tortilla.

Sprinkle cheese over chicken mixture and top with remaining tortillas.

Bake at 350 degrees for about 15 minutes, or until cheese is melted.

Serve with additional salsa, sour cream and guacamole, if you like.

Serves 3 to 4.

Start to Finish:
45 minutes

Here's a tip...

For extra zing, top Baked Mac & Cheese with salsa, nacho cheese dip or chopped green chiles.

Q: Did you hear the one about the restaurant on the moon?

A: Great food, but no atmosphere.

Baked Mac & Cheese

Ingredients

1 cup elbow macaroni

1/2 cup pasteurized process cheese sauce

2 hot dogs, chopped

 1 teaspoon grated Parmesan cheese

4 buttery round crackers, crushed

 salt and pepper to taste

Tool Kit

measuring cups & spoons ★ paring knife
stockpot ★ colander ★ 1-quart casserole dish
wooden spoon ★ microwave-safe bowl

Containers made of metal or aluminum foil will cause sparks in the microwave, so always use microwave-safe dishes. An adult can help you choose one.

Fill a stockpot with water and bring to a boil.

Add macaroni and cook for 8 to 10 minutes, stirring so it doesn't stick. Drain, using a colander.

Heat cheese sauce in microwave for one minute.

Combine cooked macaroni, cheese sauce, chopped hot dogs and Parmesan in an ungreased casserole dish using a wooden spoon.

Top with cracker crumbs and sprinkle with salt and pepper to taste.

Bake at 350 degrees for 10 minutes.

"Say Cheese"

No fruit filling here...
this pie's for dinner!

mama mia!

Easy · As · **Pie** Spaghetti Bake

Dinnertime

Serves 6.

Start to Finish:
1 hour

Make 'em mini

Instead of a pie plate, divide the ingredients into muffin cups for individual size pies.

Ingredients

1 pound ground beef

1/2 cup bread crumbs

1/2 cup onion, chopped

salt and pepper to taste

1/2 cup milk

2 cups cooked spaghetti

1 egg, beaten

1-1/2 cups spaghetti sauce

1 cup shredded mozzarella cheese

Tool Kit

measuring cups ★ paring knife ★ mixing bowls
9-inch pie plate ★ baking sheet ★ metal spatula
spoon

This recipe uses cooked spaghetti. Ask an adult for help when draining the pasta, since the steam could cause a burn.

Combine beef, bread crumbs, onion, salt, pepper and milk in a mixing bowl using your hands.

Press mixture into the bottom and up the sides of a pie plate. Place on a baking sheet.

Bake at 350 degrees for 25 minutes. If you're not sure when beef is cooked, ask an adult to check. Drain off fat. Leave the oven on since you'll be baking your pie again once it's filled.

ON TOP OF SpaGHetti, all-covered with cheese...

Mix spaghetti with beaten egg until noodles are covered. Pour into baked shell.

Top with sauce and cheese. Return to baking sheet.

Bake again for 10 minutes at 350 degrees. Remove from oven and let stand for 5 minutes.

Cut pie into wedges with spatula to serve.

39

Dinnertime

Serves 2 to 4.

Start to Finish:
30 minutes

A mini muffin tin is just right for filling with dipping sauces for these

nibblers!

Try sweet & sour sauce, spicy mustard, tangy barbecue sauce, ranch dressing and honey.

Q: What do you call a crazy chicken?

A: A cuckoo cluck.

Crispy Chicken Bites

Ingredients

2 boneless, skinless chicken breasts

1-1/2 cups seasoned bread crumbs

1/2 cup milk

non-stick vegetable spray

2 tablespoons butter, melted

salt and pepper to taste

Tool Kit

kitchen scissors ✶ measuring cups & spoons
2 cereal bowls ✶ baking sheet

40

If you have a little brother or sister close by, remember that hot baking sheets or pans should be kept where they can't be reached.

Cut chicken into 2-inch chunks using kitchen scissors. If this is too hard, ask an adult to flatten the chicken for you.

Pour bread crumbs into one cereal bowl and milk into the other one.

Dip chicken chunks into milk, then roll in crumbs to coat thoroughly.

Place in a single layer on a sprayed baking sheet.

Drizzle butter over chicken bites and sprinkle with salt and pepper.

Bake at 350 degrees for 15 to 20 minutes, or until no longer pink in the middle. If you're not sure when the chicken is done, ask an adult.

when the moon hits your eye like a big pizza pie...

Pizza 1·2·3!

Ingredients

 15-oz. can tomato sauce

1/4 cup dried, minced onion

2 teaspoons dried oregano

2 teaspoons garlic powder

 2-1/2 cups biscuit baking mix

1 env. active dry yeast 2/3 cup hot water
(120 to 130 degrees)

2 cups shredded mozzarella cheese

 toppings of your choice

Tool Kit

can opener ★ measuring cups & spoons
spoons ★ mixing bowls ★ rolling pin
baking sheet

Did You Know...?

My-oh-my
pizza pie!
Americans eat
100 acres of
pizza
per day or
350 slices
per second!

When you want to refrigerate leftovers, let them cool down a bit before placing in the refrigerator.

Stir tomato sauce, onion, oregano and garlic powder in a mixing bowl using a spoon.

Combine baking mix and yeast in a large mixing bowl. Add water gradually and stir with another spoon until thoroughly blended.

Turn out dough onto a clean, well-floured surface and knead 20 times. Allow dough to rest for 5 minutes and then divide into 3 equal parts.

Shape one part into a ball and place in the center of an ungreased baking sheet.

Roll out to 1/4-inch thick and pinch the edge to make a crust stand up around the edges.

Top with about 2/3 cup of sauce mixture and then add 1/3 of the cheese and toppings.

Bake at 425 degrees about 15 to 20 minutes, or until the crust is golden. Repeat with other dough balls to make 3 small pizzas.

Start to Finish:
30 minutes

Here's A tip...

Howdy partner! Line a cowboy hat with napkins, then fill with potato or corn chips for *snacking!*

YEEHAH!

Texas Straw Hats

Ingredients

1 pound ground beef

 1 onion, finely diced

2 tablespoons taco seasoning mix

1 tablespoon water

15-oz. bag corn chips

2 cups shredded Cheddar cheese

1/2 cup lettuce, chopped

1/2 cup tomato, chopped

1/4 cup sliced black olives

Garnish: salsa and sour cream

Tool Kit

skillet ⋆ paring knife ⋆ wooden spoon
measuring cups & spoons ⋆ colander
4 plates for serving ⋆ ice cream scoop

44

Remember not to leave boxes or bags of groceries out on the floor where they can trip up a fast-moving cook!

Crumble ground beef in a skillet. Add onion and stir well using a wooden spoon.

Cook beef mixture over medium heat until no pink remains and onion is soft. Drain, using a colander.

Return beef mixture to skillet and add seasoning and water. Stir well and simmer for 5 minutes.

Cover the bottom of 4 plates with corn chips. This is the bottom of the "hat."

Scoop out seasoned beef and onion mixture with a small ice cream scoop and place one on each plate. This makes the top of the "hat."

Divide cheese, lettuce, tomato and olives equally between all 4 servings.

Serve with salsa and sour cream on the side.

tee hee!

Dinnertime

Serves 4.

tic toc

Start to Finish:
40 minutes

Did You Know...?

The very first Ferris wheel, built in 1893, (named after bridge builder George W. Ferris), had 36 wooden cars that could each hold 60 people.

Round 'Em Up
Hot Dogs

Ingredients

7.25-oz. can coney sauce

4 hot dogs

 4 hamburger buns

8 frozen onion rings, baked

 your favorite toppings

Tool Kit

small saucepan ★ knife ★ baking sheet ★ spoon
can opener ★ spatula

While cooking on the stove, don't step away to play a game or talk on the phone. Keep your eyes on what's cookin'!

Pour coney sauce into a small saucepan and warm over low heat, stirring occasionally.

Cut 5 deep slits, 3/4 of the way through each hot dog, without cutting all the way through. Make all cuts in the same direction on the same side.

Place hot dogs on an ungreased baking sheet about 2 inches apart.

Broil 1 to 3 minutes on each side, or until hot dogs curl up into circles. Remove from oven.

Toast hamburger buns under broiler on an ungreased baking sheet for about 30 seconds.

Place hot dogs on buns and top with 2 onion rings.

Add a spoonful of coney sauce and your favorite toppings in the middle!

Dinnertime

Serves 4.

Start to Finish:
45 minutes

Here's A tip...

Line a basket with plastic, fill with soil and sprinkle with lettuce seeds. Keep watered and soon your own lettuce will be sprouting up! It's easy to tote your lettuce garden right to the kitchen.

Q: Why did the tomato blush?

A: Because it saw the salad dressing.

You're·the·Chef Salad

Ingredients

1 cucumber, peeled

1 red or yellow pepper   1 carrot, peeled

1/2 pound smoked ham, turkey or chicken

4 eggs, hardboiled and peeled

1 cup cherry tomatoes

1 head romaine lettuce, chopped

1 to 2 cups shredded Cheddar cheese

1 to 2 cups croutons

Your favorite salad dressings

Tool Kit

paring knife ✶ mini cookie cutters ✶ grater
measuring cups ✶ several serving bowls
kitchen scissors

48

*Graters are sharp...go slowly while
grating the carrot for this salad.*

Slice cucumber and pepper using a paring knife. You could also use mini cookie cutters to cut out shapes, if you like.

Grate carrot using the largest-holed section on your grater. Place in a bowl.

Cut ham, turkey or chicken and hard-boiled eggs into separate bowls using kitchen scissors.

Remove stems from cherry tomatoes and place them in a bowl.

Place lettuce, cheese and croutons in separate bowls.

Set up all the bowls of ingredients, along with your choice of dressings, salad-bar style on the table. Let everyone make their own salad!

LETTUCE

Q: What does the Invisible Man drink at snack time?
A: Evaporated milk.

← rō-teen-ie

Marzetti SwiRls

Ingredients

1 pound ground beef

1 onion, chopped

 1 tablespoon chili powder

2 teaspoons garlic powder

14-oz. can stewed tomatoes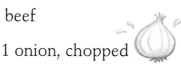

1 cup water

 1-1/2 cups rotini

Here's A tip...

Shape up! Wagon wheels, seashells, *bowties...* try all the great pasta shapes in this recipe.

Tool Kit

large lidded skillet or Dutch oven
measuring cups & spoons ★ colander
can opener ★ wooden spoon ★ paring knife

It's a good idea to leave the lid slightly off center while simmering or boiling...keeps liquid from boiling over and you can easily keep an eye on it.

Crumble ground beef into a large skillet or Dutch oven with a lid.

Add onion, chili powder and garlic powder. Stir well, using a wooden spoon, until combined.

Cook over medium-high heat for about 5 minutes, until no pink remains. Drain, using a colander.

Stir in stewed tomatoes and water. Bring to boil.

Simmer with a lid on for 5 minutes.

Stir in rotini. Put the lid back on and continue to simmer 10 to 12 minutes, or until rotini is tender.

6

Serves 6 to 8.

tic toc

Start to Finish:
30 minutes

Here's A tip...

Picture-perfect parfaits...made any way you want! Try peanut butter or crumbled chocolate chip cookies and any flavor pudding...you can't go wrong!

Pink Peppermint Parfaits

OOOH La La!

Ingredients

3.4-oz. pkg. instant vanilla pudding mix

1/4 teaspoon peppermint extract

8-oz. container frozen whipped topping, thawed

1-1/2 cups milk

3 drops red food coloring

6 chocolate sandwich cookies

6 candy canes

Tool Kit

measuring cups & spoons ★ mixing bowl
electric mixer ★ wooden spoon
plastic zipping bag ★ rolling pin
parfait or drinking glasses

*Food coloring can stain clothes and some countertops,
so squeeze the bottles gently.*

Mix pudding mix and milk as directed on the box using an electric mixer.

Add peppermint extract and food coloring to blended pudding, mixing in with an electric mixer.

Fold in whipped topping with a wooden spoon.

Place cookies and candy canes in a gallon-size plastic zipping bag.

Roll over the cookies and candy with a rolling pin carefully until they are crumbly enough to sprinkle. Shake the bag to combine.

Layer cookie and candy crumbles and then pudding mixture in tall parfait glasses or even drinking glasses, starting and ending with crumbles.

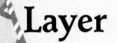

Ode to my parfait:

*I love my French fries,
I love my French toast.
But pink peppermint parfaits
Are what I love the most!*

What teacher wouldn't love a basket of these apple-filled treats? Tie a mini chalkboard on the *basket* handle as a To/From tag.

G'day mate! There really was a Granny Smith who discovered a new apple seedling growing on her farm in Australia!

Apple-Cinnamon Turnovers

Ingredients

 3 apples, cored, peeled and diced

1 cup brown sugar, packed

3 tablespoons all-purpose flour

3/4 teaspoon cinnamon

1/4 teaspoon nutmeg

2 8-oz. tubes refrigerated crescent rolls

 2 tablespoons milk

3/4 cup powdered sugar

Tool Kit

paring knife ⋆ measuring cups & spoons
mixing bowls ⋆ wooden spoon ⋆ baking sheet
spoon ⋆ fork ⋆ whisk

54

An apple peeler makes quick work of peeling apples!

Mix diced apples with brown sugar, flour, cinnamon and nutmeg.

Separate crescent rolls on the dotted lines and place half of them on an ungreased baking sheet.

Spoon 1 to 2 tablespoons of apple mixture in center of each crescent roll. Top each with another triangle of dough.

Seal edges of dough together using a fork to crimp.

Bake at 350 degrees for 12 to 15 minutes.

Whisk milk and powdered sugar together until smooth.

Drizzle glaze over each turnover while still hot.

Serves 8 to 10.

VROOM

Start to Finish:
15 minutes

Here's a tip...

Not just for
Halloween...
gross 'em out
any time!
Top cups with
gummy frogs,
sharks, snakes
or crocodiles.

EEWWW! Gross

Guaranteed to GROSS OUT grown-ups!

Cups of Dirt with Worms

Ingredients

3.9-oz. pkg. instant chocolate pudding mix

2 cups milk

8-oz. container frozen whipped topping, thawed

16-oz. pkg. chocolate sandwich cookies

8 to 10 7-oz. plastic cups

gummy worms

Tool Kit

measuring cups ✶ mixing bowl ✶ electric mixer
plastic zipping bag ✶ rolling pin ✶ spoon

*Set a rolling pin back in its holder or on a dishcloth
to keep it from rolling off the counter.*

Mix pudding mix and milk as directed on the box using an electric mixer. Fold in whipped topping.

Place 8 to 10 cookies in a gallon-size plastic zipping bag.

Roll over the cookies with a rolling pin carefully until they are crumbly but not crushed. Repeat with remaining cookies.

Place a spoonful of cookie crumbles in the bottom of each cup.

Fill cups half-full with pudding mixture. Top with more cookies and repeat until cups are full.

Decorate with gummy worms and enjoy!

Makes 20 cookies.

tic toc

Start to Finish:
1 hour

Did You Know...?

It's said these yummy cookies originated in Germany where they were called schneckennudeln... it's just that the name has changed over many, many years!

Q: Why did the cookie go to the doctor?

A: He was feeling crumby.

snicker poodle →

Shickerdoodles

Snickerdoodle Cookies

Ingredients

BUTTER — 1 cup butter

1-1/2 cups sugar   2 eggs, beaten

1 teaspoon vanilla extract

2-3/4 cups all-purpose flour   (not those!) ←

2 teaspoons cream of tartar

1 teaspoon baking soda

2 tablespoons sugar

2 teaspoons cinnamon

Tool Kit

measuring cups & spoons ★ mixing bowls
whisk ★ fork ★ cereal bowl ★ baking sheet
spatula ★ cooling rack ★ wooden spoon

Be sure to set a timer for baking time for yummy, not burned, cookies!

Mix butter and 1-1/2 cups of sugar together in a large mixing bowl. Add beaten eggs and vanilla.

Combine flour, cream of tartar and baking soda in another mixing bowl.

Add flour mixture to the butter mixture a little at a time until the dough is blended and no flour is left in the bottom of the bowl.

Combine remaining sugar and cinnamon with a fork in cereal bowl.

Roll dough into balls and toss in cinnamon-sugar. Place on an ungreased baking sheet.

Bake at 400 degrees for 8 to 10 minutes, or until they're puffy and edges are golden. Cool on a wire rack 5 minutes.

Makes 6 pops.

Start to Finish:
25 minutes

Turn 'em into
friends &
family! Leave
off the cookie,
then add
wax lips,
jelly bean eyes
and string
licorice whips
for hair!

Crispie
MonKey
Pops

Ingredients

3 tablespoons butter

4 cups mini marshmallows

6 cups crispy rice cereal

12 vanilla wafers

12 brown candy-coated chocolates

6 red jelly beans

6 chocolate-filled oval sandwich cookies

1 cup chocolate frosting

1 tube brown decorating gel

non-stick vegetable spray

Tool Kit

measuring cups ✲ saucepan ✲ 13"x9" baking pan
spatula ✲ circle or oval cookie cutter ✲ wax paper
lollipop sticks ✲ wooden spoon ✲ butter knife

60

It's a good idea to put hot saucepans in the sink so they don't accidentally get pulled off the countertop or stove.

Melt butter in a large saucepan over low heat. Add marshmallows and stir until melted.

Add crispy rice cereal and stir to coat. Remove from heat.

Pat into a sprayed baking pan with the back of a spatula sprayed with non-stick vegetable spray. Try to get the mixture as flat as possible.

Cut mixture with a circle or oval cookie cutter. Lift out carefully and set on a sheet of wax paper to cool slightly. Insert lollipop sticks.

Spread frosting with a butter knife on vanilla wafers to "glue" onto back of circle or oval as shown to make ears. Use frosting to "glue" on candy-coated chocolates, jelly beans and sandwich cookies. Spread frosting on top of monkey pop as shown.

Squeeze decorating gel on sandwich cookie to make mouth.

Q: What's a monkey's favorite cookie?

A: Chocolate chimp.

Beverage

Serves 2 to 4.

tic toc

Start to Finish:
1 hour

Turn your hollowed-out watermelon from this recipe into a beat-the-heat cooler! Just fill with crushed ice and juice boxes.

Try saying this tongue-twister ten times fast!
Lenny Lion likes licking lemon lollipops.

Lemonade 25¢

Melonberry Lemonade

Ingredients

6 cups watermelon, cubed and seeded

 1/2 cup raspberries

1 cup water

1/2 cup sugar

1/2 cup lemon juice

Tool Kit

measuring cups ★ blender ★ strainer
1 or 2-quart pitcher ★ rubber spatula
long-handled spoon

Wash all fruits and vegetables before eating.
Use just clear, clean water and no soap.

Combine watermelon, raspberries and water in blender. Ask an adult to help out.

Blend until smooth.

Pour through a strainer into pitcher.

Push liquid through with a rubber spatula when draining slows down.

Stir sugar and lemon juice into strained mixture until sugar dissolves.

Chill about 30 minutes or serve over ice.

Dessert

Serves 2 to 4.

Start to Finish:
10 minutes

Berry-delicious fruit straws... slide strawberry and banana slices onto drinking straws, then put one in each glass. Scrumptious!

Q: What did the raspberry say to the blueberry?

A: I love you berry, berry much!

Very **Berry** Smoothies

Ingredients

3/4 cup blueberries

3/4 cup raspberries

1-1/4 cup vanilla yogurt   1/4 cup milk

1/2 teaspoon vanilla extract

Tool Kit

measuring cups & spoons ★ blender

Frozen fruit is super in smoothies too!
No need to thaw berries, just toss 'em in the blender
with all the other ingredients.

Combine all ingredients in a blender. Ask an adult to help out.

Blend until smooth. Pour into glasses to serve.

The tree of smoothie

Serves 1.

VROOM

Start to Finish:
5 minutes

Here's a tip...

Shake it up...try peanut butter swirl ice cream or peanut butter-chocolate. Make shakes extra special with a dollop of whipped cream and a cherry!

PB&J Milkshakes

Ingredients

2 tablespoons peanut butter

3 tablespoons your favorite jelly

1/2 cup milk

1 cup vanilla ice cream

Tool Kit

measuring cups & spoons ⋆ spoon ⋆ cereal bowl
ice cream scoop ⋆ blender

Tighten the lid on the blender to keep your milkshake from splattering everywhere!

Stir peanut butter and jelly together in a cereal bowl.

Place milk and ice cream in a blender.

Add peanut butter and jelly.

Blend until smooth. Ask an adult to help out.

THUMP
tHUMP.

tic toc

Start to Finish:
30 minutes

Did You Know...?

Even a cupcake can be a tongue-twister. Try saying this fast!

A cupcake cook in a cupcake cook's cap cooks cupcakes.

Cupcake Creations

Ingredients

baked cupcakes, icing, decorating gel, round white mint candies, chocolate chips, gumdrops, chocolate-covered peanut butter cups, almonds, mini chocolate chips, vanilla wafers, mini candy-coated chocolates, coarse sugar, candy-coated chocolates, mini marshmallows

cat

Frost cupcakes with white frosting.

ears

Add eyes with 2 green candy-coated chocolates and ears by cutting a mini marshmallow in half diagonally.

Finish whiskers with lines of black decorating gel and nose and insides of ears with pink decorating gel.

68

OWL

Frost cupcake with white icing.

Add eyes for head by piping white icing into the center hole of a round white mint candy; insert a chocolate chip in the hole of the candy. Attach eyes to peanut butter cup using white frosting.

Cut a yellow gumdrop into a triangle for the nose. Secure to peanut butter cup with white frosting.

Place two almonds, secured with white frosting, on the back of the chocolate-covered peanut butter cup for ears.

Push chocolate-covered peanut butter cup into cupcake.

Finish by placing 2 vanilla wafers on each side of the cupcake for wings and several chocolate chips to create the feathered chest.

FROG

Frost cupcakes with green frosting.

Add eyes by piping white icing onto the bottom of a green gumdrop; place a green mini candy-coated chocolate in the center of the frosting. Add a mouth by piping on green decorating gel.

Finish with a sprinkling of coarse sugar.

Just for Fun

Makes 2 cups.

Start to Finish:
30 minutes

Toothpicks can
turn clay into
curly tails and
tongues, while a
garlic press makes
wonderful hair
(better ask first
before using!)

Curly
tail

toothpick

Super Sweet

PlayClay

Ingredients

1/3 cup margarine, softened

 1/3 cup corn syrup

1/4 teaspoon salt

1 teaspoon vanilla extract

16-oz. pkg. powdered sugar

assorted food coloring

Tool Kit

measuring cups & spoons ✳ rubber spatula
mixing bowl ✳ airtight storage container

So that you can have plenty of fun the next time, store your clay with the lid securely on the airtight container so the clay won't harden!

Mix margarine, corn syrup, salt and vanilla extract in a mixing bowl with a rubber spatula.

Add powdered sugar a little at a time and mix with your hands.

Add more corn syrup if the mixture is too dry.

Divide clay into smaller parts and add a few drops of food coloring to make whatever colors you like.

Store and keep chilled in an airtight storage container once you're done playing with it.

to make a tutu, fold a long strip of clay back and forth.

The secret for super-size bubbles is to store this bubble mix in the fridge overnight.

Giant Bubble Mix

Ingredients

4 cups water

2 cups liquid dish soap

2 cups glycerin (sold in drug stores)

2 teaspoons corn syrup

Tool Kit

measuring cups & spoons ★ large shallow pan
wooden spoon ★ wire hanger or cotton string

72

Need help bending the hanger to make your bubble wand?
Please ask an adult to help or use a loop of string instead!

Pour all ingredients into a shallow pan.

Stir mixture slowly until it's combined.

Bend hanger into a square, circle or any closed shape. You can also use a loop of cotton string, if you like.

Dip hanger or string loop into bubble mixture and lift out gently.

Blow or wave the wand to make bubbles. You can also run and watch the bubbles come out behind you! Pour into an airtight container to store.

Makes 1 cup.

VROOM

Start to Finish:
15 minutes

Here's
A tip...

Lions, tigers &
bears...oh, my!
You can even use
mini heart, star
or flower-shaped
stencils to make
face painting
oh-so easy.

Homemade

Face paint

Ingredients

1/2 cup cornstarch

1/4 cup cold cream

1/4 cup water

assorted food coloring

Tool Kit

measuring cups ✶ mixing bowl ✶ spoon
small bowls ✶ plastic zipping bags

To keep face paint fresh squeeze any excess air out of the plastic zipping bags.

Mix cornstarch and cold cream together and stir until they are well blended.

Stir in water. This is your face paint base.

Divide face paint base into as many small bowls as you like, depending on how many colors you want to make.

Add food coloring one drop at a time and stir well.

Store paint in plastic zipping bags.

Just for Fun

Makes 1 dozen.

Start to Finish:
1 hour

Dog-gone-it... Fido deserves a treat too! Fill a jar with these biscuits, then tie on a new leash for the bow!

Barking Buddy

Dog Biscuits

Ingredients

2 cups whole-wheat flour

3/4 cup all-purpose flour

1/3 cup cornmeal

1 teaspoon garlic powder

 1/2 teaspoon salt

1/4 cup oats 1/4 cup molasses

2 tablespoons vegetable oil

2 eggs, beaten   1/2 cup milk

non-stick vegetable spray

Tool Kit

mixing bowl ★ wooden spoon ★ rolling pin
measuring cups & spoons ★ cookie cutters
baking sheet

Place a non-stick baking mat on your baking sheet…treats slide right off!

Mix all the dry ingredients in a large mixing bowl.

Stir in molasses, oil, eggs and milk until dough sticks together and there's no powder left.

Roll dough out on a well-floured surface to a 1/2-inch thickness.

Cut out biscuits with your favorite cookie cutters.

Place biscuits on a sprayed baking sheet and bake at 350 degrees for 30 minutes.

Turn the oven off, but leave biscuits in the oven for another 20 more minutes to harden.

Fido

Just for Fun

Makes 1-1/2 cups.

VROOM

Start to Finish:
10 minutes

Here's
a tip...

Goo, Goop,
Slime...whatever
you call it, it's
birthday party or
rainy-day fun...

guaranteed!

Goopy Goo (not Boo!)

Ingredients

1 cup all-purpose white glue GLUE

1 cup water, divided

food coloring

1 tablespoon borax

Tool Kit

measuring cups and spoons ★ metal spoon
bowls ★ plastic zipping bags

78

Add the food coloring just a drop at time
until you get the exact color you want.

Blend together glue and 3/4 cup water in a large bowl; stir until smooth.

Add desired amount of food coloring; blend well and set aside.

Blend remaining water with borax in a small bowl; stir well.

Add contents of small bowl to glue mixture; stir until goo begins to form, then remove from bowl. There will be some liquid remaining in the bowl.

Make another batch of goo by blending 1/4 cup water with borax in a small bowl.

Add to the remaining liquid in the first bowl; stir until goo begins to form.

Store goo in plastic zipping bags.

Here we go goopy GOO,
Here we go goopy gie...

How did **Gooseberry Patch** get started?

Since '84, we've been together
Two country friends,

birds of a feather
who talked across the back-
yard fence…now, skip ahead
to present tense:

A small idea we first hatched
has grown into **Gooseberry Patch**.

We've sent cookie cutters,
books by the ton

Time does fly when you're having FUN!

But the nicest part along the way
are the folks we hear from every day
phone calls, recipes,
cards & letters
about the times
friends spend together.

So spend some time with us again
We're proud to have you as a friend!

Nickie & JoAnn

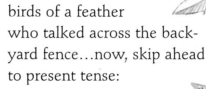